CW00487350

DADA

CUNT*

now that i have your attention, let's talk about art, cringe, and the internet

First published by Dawid Tysowski 2021

Copyright © 2021 by dada

All rights reserved. No part of this publication may be reproduced, stored or transmitted in any form or by any means, electronic, mechanical, photocopying, recording, scanning, or otherwise without written permission from the publisher. It is illegal to copy this book, post it to a website, or distribute it by any other means without permission.

First edition

This book was professionally typeset on Reedsy. Find out more at reedsy.com

I

ART

since I've seen the dark
and light burns in my heart
I become – art

ART

Surely, many have tried to define art, and so many of them have failed miserably - or at least so we can tell in retrospect. In this little chapbook, you will find no definite answers, sometimes not even vague answers at all. Quoting Lyotard, the difference between an expert and a philosopher is that the former knows what they know and what they don't know (so they know their shit), while the latter only questions, doubts, and tries to break apart.

In these postmodern times, it's hard to define any-thing, as a matter of fact, but art is one of these things that are just entertaining (brain food, if you may) to talk, think, or write about.

Our daily reality, our perception, is a controlled hallucination constructed by social standards and agreements between people, rooted deep in our unconscious minds throughout our childhood and upbringing, as well as our physical perceptive capabilities. Culture is but an imposed simulation that developed through history. Some see it as a development of nature, others prefer to distinguish man from nature and hence deem culture *unnatural*.

One's identity and behaviour too are a simulation of ego, which is created artificially. Whether the process is conscious or not – or to what extent – depends on the level of one's self-awareness. The way we act is a result of our environment and circumstances, with just the illusion of free will (the degree of our free will is still a major dispute in my head without any resolutions on the horizon) – and we act a certain way to get a desired response from other people, from society.

In today's interconnected world of the internet, social media are a digital extension of the societal spectacle. By creating our social media accounts, what we do is construct one or more digital avatars – in other words, we create egos which are always out there for people to see, even when we're not engaged in the social spectacle at the moment. Especially among the youth, social media platforms are one's business card for popularity, aesthetic, and so on.

So, online, people can make a judgement of us even if we're not actively participating. For this reason, so many of us are so thoughtful with the content we upload. As time passes, old pictures that no longer match our current identity are simply ditched.

Even if you don't care how others perceive you, in itself it's a response you want to get - so the content you upload (e.g. cringe or ugly pictures of yourself) is to leave people thinking, "Oh, this one really doesn't care." It's all about seeding an idea in the minds of other people.

Take this book as an example - the structure is not too strict, not all of this makes sense, not even all of this is what I actually think sometimes. All my philosophy books are messy, sometimes with a couple of layers of irony on them. There is an idea behind chaos.

<|>

Art is a religion and creating something is a ritual. It provides one with a sense of individual unity with oneself and clicking into the (collective and personal) unconscious, operating in the metaphysical realm devoid of ego. Like every other ritual (a mass, a meeting with friends, a concert), it is nonredeemable time devoted to something deeper, as time is all we really have.

Confusing reality with fiction has lately been a sorta gimmick of mine. I will say openly that all of my works could be categorised as *autobiographical fiction* - but then on the other hand, isn't all art deriving inspiration from the creator's own experiences? Whether they lay the cards in the open is a whole different question.

Such an approach to one's art is just identity creation, and when there is some unclarity, it makes the audience all the more interested. People want to know what is true, honest, or genuine, but nothing ever fully is. All we can do is create a temporary expression of the soul's infinity, but what we create is just an artificial reproduction of an idea, and a poem is perfect only in the poet's head.

So, when it comes to an artist's actions, while the audience is so often preoccupied with finding out the truth, the artist may say that truth doesn't really matter. Why care if this or that anecdote *actually* happened, if it's all a matter of interpretation, which is in itself subjective and by no means guarantees an idea's validity.

When it comes to ideas, it's not other people's recognition that gives them validity, but the sole premise of their existence. If it came to your head, then it *is* -

and sometimes that's enough.

<|>

There is a feeling of boredom in today's late-capitalist culture that perpetrates me. Everything looks the same, every successful movie becomes a franchise, and all the industries care about is whether something sells. What we lack is the courage to experiment, to make new, to surprise.

I've observed various content creators on TikTok (writing this late 2021, I wonder how soon this particular social media app becomes obsolete), and the formula is commonly shared: you begin with a few different forms of content, and when one of them gets more popular, you focus more and more on that one type of content, and in the end (especially when it comes to comedy TikToks) all you do is sell the same product in a slightly different package, you focus on views more than the content itself, and everything is a copy of a copy. Even if the content was original or even experimental in the beginning (maybe it was a parody of something, a catchphrase), its only function now is referring to itself, existing in that meta-ironic sphere of mechanical reproduction without room for stylistic development.

Case study: a TikTok whence a guy is in the kitchen with his parents. The guy tells a pick-up line kinda joke (which has to do with sex but not deliberately). Then the dad follows up with another joke, and the mum doesn't get it. It looks like a random familial interaction caught on camera – at first! When you see the very same structure (guy tells a joke, dad follows up, mum doesn't understand) repeated over and over again, it becomes repetitive and predictable – but it still sells, and oh, it sells even better!

This is a predicament of capitalism, not the creatives themselves. Experimentation is possible, but it is risky.

<|>

There is no better challenge than a challenge against my old self - trying to put together words more profound, draw finer lines, make music that speaks deeper to the heart - and break all the dams I've put up and push for new tides; be a terrorist and provoke, destabilise, piss off, disgust, astonish, make somebody cringe, make them run away.

Once you've established yourself in the industry, you get more room for experimentation and freedom of expression. I like those experimental little touches added to highly commercial products, just like "I Love Kanye" on "The Life of Pablo." I'm not sure about Kanye's intent behind the song, but my impression is that he just wanted to prove that something like that *can* exist - and indeed it does. It's not something you'd particularly enjoy, to some it's just stupid, but hey - it's there, and it's out there.

<|>

Among anti-capitalist artists and activists, the struggle is between going off the grid (not participating in the capitalist dynamic) and spreading anti-capitalist ideas through newspapers, art, or other propagandist, mass-media industries. Because capitalism does such a good job at incorporating any protest against it into one of its branches to profit from, counterculture folks have had troubles putting the two things together (I don't want to participate in capitalism, but I also want to sell my art so that I can live off of it).

Some engage in business, capitalist enterprises to promote anti-capitalist propaganda; which is something that anti-capitalist activists have always been doing but what they can't face. And, surely, it's something that bothered me for a while too. Yet, the contradiction (fuck capitalism - shot on an iPhone) is not necessarily hypocrisy and doesn't exclude itself - on the contrary, it covers the entire spectrum and provides a holistic, objective (i.e. striving towards objectivity, surely achieving it is hardly possible, if at all, given all the variables...) outlook on the situation.

With the expansion of capitalism, we see a relative expansion of anti-capitalist values. In the spirit of capitalist realism and cultural accelerationism, some postmodern thinkers claim that by speeding up the systemic money machine, we will lead it to a breakdown.

I've been challenged on this particular viewpoint, that it's just an excuse not to take immediate action and keep exploiting the working class. But, if you want to lead society to a revolution, what else you gonna do? Stay in your squat on the fringes of society? You might see it as morally superior, but does in fact very little for propagating revolutionary ideas.

And we have to be all in this together to make a change.

To give humans a collective identity we must see our species and society not as a group (so a collection of people that share certain traits, e.g. based on race, sex, gender, or sexuality) but as an anti-group, a collection of diverse individuals whose identity is of no inherent value but exists only as an essenceless manifestation intertwined with a social setting and temporal qualities. Instead of looking for the things that connect us, let's embrace our differences and celebrate diversity beyond identity politics, in a collective struggle for the individual.

Another thing worth mentioning is that the working class may just not have the energy to take up their torches. After hours of work a day, there's little mental and physical capacity left to take up a draining task, even such as questioning the validity of their everyday reality. We don't need gladiators anymore; we've got television.

In many revolutionary and counter-cultural movements of today, activists push for the rejection of economic growth as a moral obligation to humanity - an approach of opposing means to embracing hopelessness, yet one with identical ends. Yet, no matter one's anti-capitalist beliefs, all counterculture and revolutionary movements get incorporated into the system anyway: from Nirvana, through AdBusters, to any anarchist collective that want to reach a wider audience. They all use social media to communicate, drive cars to move about, and not just utilise, but *need* capital in order to go on. That's capitalist realism. Nevertheless, I am willing to entertain the idea that while the hopeless culture of late capitalism is being pushed to its limit, some circles organise and get ready for a revolution to come.

<| >

Art is one of the mediums to propagate ideas in the heads of the public. What is art? What are the differences between fashion and fast fashion? Are cheap clothes from Primark a form of art? Where are the borders, if they're there?

Sometimes I get thoughts of letting it all go and spending the rest of my life in a monastery or a sustainable farm but it's not my kind of aesthetic yet.

When everyone can post anything and call it truth, what is real or factual no longer plays such an important role - and we all know that what most people see as facts are but a warped version of reality, shaped by mass media and the people behind it. Hence, instead of fighting misinformation, which is a task far too difficult for us to ever tackle (especially with the rise of deepfake and AI), a form of artistic expression in post-truth postmodernity is to become misinformation, to be a sort of online troll and create fake news just for the hell of it, as we've seen a couple of years ago with *Breitbart*.

The phenomenon of alternative right is a curious thing to see. Our neo-liberal politicians lack a coherent version of a different, better future, which leads the right to radicalise - which is clear in the rise of Donald Trump in the US or conservatives in Europe. Right-wingers have a higher ground over neo-liberals as they provide security in the now, and do it all the more efficiently by intertwining populist social policies that satisfy the masses in the short term.

I see Milo Yiannapoulous as a great hoaxer, an artist worthy of our time - to what extent his alt-right politics as a gay man are genuine is a question of speculations, for the magician never reveals their tricks - to me it seems that Milo embraces the cultural hopelessness in the spirit of capitalist realism and extremisizes (?) the right to motivate a new, third, revolutionary force to enter the political stage.

It's (it might be) similar to Slavoj Žižek supporting Trump or Peretti's BuzzFeed business model that, despite contradictory actions, indirectly acts in favour of anti-capitalist motives.

<|>

Writing as therapy – released suppressed emotions and letting the unconscious (creativity) loose to prevent Freudian neurosis (every emotion not expressed becomes neurosis) – it's just a *different* way of expressing emotions – When I speak up, they laugh. When I don't, they say I'm closed off... and I'd rather be seen as an outcast than a laughing stock.

<|>

The interdisciplinisation of one's talent is a good way of preventing the writer's (the creator's) block. There are many ways of channeling genius, and if the mind is (at the moment) infertile for poetry, it might be fit for music or digital art or memes.

The only guilt I ever feel is if I don't spend some time creating – or do I really? Am I not just saying it to justify my existence somehow?

A couple days without a paragraph written or a poem put together or even a note in a notebook taken down – a mark left – and suddenly I'm overtaken by a grim darkness, a lifeless numbness, and physical pain in the abdomen.

We humans (contemporary society) tend to find the most sympathy and appreciation towards artists only when they're dead. Maybe their genius is less intimidating to the general population and they can say: look, he was no god, he was just like the rest of us.

Creation is leaving a mark after yourself, it's giving life to something the universe hasn't seen yet.

Are memes art? Is shitposting a form of art? I remember from history classes the protests against abstract paintings. Conservatives saying it's not art because breaks all ideas of what we used to call art. In the age of mechanical reproduction, originality is no longer so valued, and something *making sense* is no longer a factor for its importance. Memes embrace the absurdity of existence, as chaotic art meets technology.

I used to think that every story, every piece of art, could be summarised in one sentence, as its essence, and that stories are a way to transcend lore into something metaphysical yet easy to understand, something memorable despite its complexity. I still think that it may be like that in many cases, but that the essence is subjective: to some, the life of Jesus can be a gospel of and an ode to serfdom, while to others it will be a glorification of freedom... And who is there to decide who's right or wrong? Jesus? Or any of the evangelists? Maybe their therapists? Paradoxically, isn't there freedom in submission?

When a poet writes or a painter paints, for them it's also the first time they see their work, they see an expression of the absolute of infinite possibilities take shape. It's like you're both the reader and the listener, the creator and the consumer - or sometimes a whole audience.

I have to write. Otherwise I'm miserable and I might as well die. If I don't create and give something to the world, then why am I even alive for? This is a deal I made with God.

Art as the ultimate expression of God: What is God? I'm not a fan of old dudes in the skies and wicked monsters in the ground. God is the void, it is nothingness with the infinite potential to become anything, and any creation is an expression of what nothingness can be. All of us humans are the same omnipotent consciousness that experiences itself subjectively, shaped by our experiences and so on, which then brings up all these different thoughts that come to us, which for some reason we identify as ourselves.

Discussing God, the divine, or the meaning of the universe is more often than not a problem of language. Trying to provide all-inclusive answers on any given topic is extremely difficult not just because of the overwhelming complexity of reality (both social, personal, or whichever framework we prefer to choose), but also because of the *paradoxical nature* of reality. You see, there seems to be something metaphysically clicking with paradoxes, with accepting seemingly opposing statements not as contradictions, but inextricable parts of the whole. Language, as a human creation, seems incapable of delivering a paradoxical statement without it sounding like gibberish, which is why comprehension of such notions as that of submission to the flow of the universe versus individual freedom or free will (that is, true freedom lies in submission) requires the belief factor, the leap of faith that conveys a simple message: I know this is true, but I have no clue how to explain that to you.

Imagine you say *enlightenment* and everyone knows what you're talking about, with a vivid image in their heads or a feeling in their stomachs, like when you say *house* or *apple*.

To contradict the usual religious narratives, present in religions such as Christianity or Judaism as well as new age spirituality, I prefer to talk about *deeper* levels of consciousness instead of *higher* ones. This hierarchical outlook on enlightenment has been a major part of theology, perhaps because our societies depended (and still do) on interhuman hierarchies, whence someone is the master and the other one the slave. Similarly, psychoanalysis put the unconscious in Oedipal hierarchies, implying that the family structure not just is but *has to be* hierarchical, as we go through life with patriarchal fathers or bosses, generation after generation. Yet, the unconscious is an omnipotent machine, and Oedipus, feudalism, or capitalism are just frameworks that we force onto it. All that's profound, creative, divine, does not come from the skies - although the skies might be a compelling metaphor, and likely have been to people a thousand years ago without any knowledge on meteorology etc. - but from within, from the depths of the unconscious.

When you meditate, you begin to notice that you don't really choose your thoughts or feelings - they come to you, and the more you explore those depths, the more you realise just how deep they go and how little we know.

The metaphor of the skies or even the universe out there disconnects humans from that vital force devoid of time and space. One's journey must lead from being submissive to an outer divine force to finding it within oneself, through challenging and becoming a god and equal to all humans, subsequently to understanding we're one with all humans, as we're all that infinitely potent void put in different circumstances and experiencing itself subjectively.

Art as an entity whose only goal is experimental production, a momentary expression of the self.

Art as provocation, a roar of uprising whose only goal is to raise controversy and break the rules just for the hell of it.

I think we have free will to say no (to the flow of universe, to the production of the unconscious (hence repression hysteria/paranoia)?

For example: I don't really choose to create, it bursts out of me. But I could choose not to create, to let go of the ideas that come to me forever - but I don't, for what other reason to live could I ever find? And even that seems laughable sometimes. There is no better challenge than a challenge against the old me, a glove thrown spitefully into the face of my past self - but I've already said that, haven't I?

II

CRINGE

imma leave y'all howling
imma make y'all bereft
for you can't unsee
the ego death

CRINGE

Just 5 years ago, I remember, mullet was the cringest, most laughable hairstyle - so often we laughed at pictures from the nineties, and asked ourselves, "Did people really think that was cool?" And I laughed at it too. Today, again, the hairstyle gains popularity, and out of the blue I just like it. Trends, fashion, what is deemed "cool" or "cringe" is to a large extent a matter of peer pressure. "Our" tastes are in fact influenced by the content we consume and our environment. Who is there to decide what is "good taste," what looks good? Since everything is a social construct, and our free will is but an illusion, doing things that go against common sense, things that are offensive, disgusting, cringe, or mad, is a form of a revolutionary art that requires plenty of courage.

Today's perception of cringe and cringe artists is just a new form of kitsch - so art whose goal it is to be disliked by the general population, and those artists are people of enlightenment, fully detached from how others perceive them, from their ego. Cringe is a form of a detachment from ego - take Eric Andre as an example, whose jokes are offensive and who is not afraid to talk about masturbation, sex, or feces on his show.

Cringe is nothing new. Cringe is just a contemporary development of what kitsch used to represent, standing up against the illusions that so many of us take for granted. I saw a meme with Buddha who said, "When I accept the fact that I was cringe, I was able to embrace my true self." The enlightened one just is, detached from ego (how others perceive them), careless about societal standards, wearing Crocs and mullets, enjoying life devoid of anxieties and insecurities of the 'normal people.'

< | >

In postmodernity, following Nietzsche's ideas that nothing is true and morality is relative, the morality of humour in relation to free speech has been a hot topic across social media. The so-called cancel-culture is always on the lookout for celebrities who slip a prejudiced line and call them out, as if we hadn't already known that what we see on television is but an artificial creation of a perfect celebrity-being.

How the turntables. Now, it's the right (Right?) who isn't afraid of trolling and the left who cares about safe spaces where no one can be offended. But the point of a fact is, some people are offended by anything. What we say is just a meta-ironic, meaningless pointing out of a thought's, an idea's existence - what the other person does with our words, then, is beyond our control, no matter how many apology posts we write.

And let's be frank - if a celebrity says something homophobic or racist, and then they apologise for it, it doesn't mean they actually regret what they've said - they're just trying to save their face.

And a face is oh so important, so symbolic, especially in the times of a global pandemic. New social boundaries are created, where the rich enjoy their privileges like nothing happened, while the servant working class has to hide behind masks and follow all the more absurd laws that create only the illusion of safety from an illusory threat. The COVID-19 restrictions are a simulated reality, aimed at making people live in fear to remain obedient and dependent on the state and mass media.

But let's get back to the morality of humour - especially dark, edgy, and offensive comedy, with comedians such as Ricky Gervais, Jimmy Carr, or Eric Andre. Jokes about the Holocaust, about paedophilia, about tragic events in the recent history such as 9/11 - all of these are a result of how absurd modern living is (and memes as comedy are an important part of it). We live our everyday lives, worrying about the paycheck and groceries, only to get back home and watch a television broadcast about military conflicts in the Middle East, about the nuclear threats of North Korea, about millions of children starving worldwide. Human suffering is so ubiquitous, yet - because we can't directly experience it - all we get is a detached simulation, a collection of images and opinions, all of which are thoughtfully moulded to fit some political agenda.

Questioning reality and everything we know leads to controversy, and in the artistic sphere Eric Andre defies rule after rule. What is disgusting, what is offensive, what is taboo? The answer is not so simple, as our ideas of what is what are largely influenced by societal norms into which we've been born. Important to point this out, not all of the societal standards are necessarily useless - though they do play a role in limiting our perception into pre-made frameworks, a lot of them are meant to keep society as vast as ours in control to provide a sense of security for the general populace. This is a justification of power and control: we have to trust our rulers, because their control over us grants us stability. But - surely there is a but - such justification is a philosophical matter of human nature. What is the fundamental value that permeates humanity: security or liberty? Because if we put freedom at the very bottom of our pyramid, then state power loses the validation of its power. The reason why people like Eric Andre with his stupid jokes and pranks is to make us think that the way we perceive reality is just a construction, and not the only one but indeed one of many. Likewise in politics, we've grown to see the political stage as a choice between left and right, between reactionary conservatives and pseudo-progressive liberals, while the political spectrum is in fact a vast plain. Why is there no capitalist anarchist party, no fascist party, no world unification party, no world annihilation party?

Who made the decision that we should see reality in terms of disgusting or not, or - fundamentally - right and wrong? There is no objective truth, and each action can be perceived as either or. Hence, everything you say or do has no inherent value in itself, and it's meaning can only be assessed subjectively, temporarily, and often in retrospect.

History doesn't exist. Whether you're a terrorist or

a revolutionary is a matter of opinion, and the past is now only used as a means to justify the legitimacy of those in power. Think of how Columbus has been glorified in the Western culture, how America itself has become the herald of the "civilised world" and "progress," while its crimes have been successfully avoided in history books and labelled taboo. On the other hand, history can also be used as a contradictory means, aimed at undermining the legitimacy of power. The idea that we can learn from the lessons of history is a magnificent one, yet by questioning history, by noticing how it is but a whore for ideology (either mainstream or counter-cultural) stirs a great confusion in our heads.

Ego death and cringe seem inextricably intertwined to me. Once we detach from ego, from others' perception of us, we're truly free to follow all our whims without second thought. For the extent to which we can control how we're perceived is no longer something to bother us, as we simply stop caring about it. When doing something disgusting or cringe, it's not *me* per se, it's my ego to which somebody can relate. The "I" remains intact and is truly unattainable. The soul, the divine, floats freely in the void, in a dimension completely disconnected from what most people take for granted as truth or reality.

Genius is close to madness. Sometimes it's one with a little bit of the other, but you can never really tell.

Divine mania was a concept that developed a couple of thousand years ago. This practice was known among sages, philosophers, or shamans - people with a great amount of self-awareness who shaped their behaviour in a way that a regular by-stander would instantly interpret as mental illness. There is something inherently mad about it, something insane, to play with people's perception of ourselves just for the hell of it, making people think we're crazy when we're actually not.

"They don't know I'm not crazy! They really must think I'm mad!" he exclaimed, and all you could see was that impish touch of insanity in his iris.

Intriguing to see how many of our actions are just for the aesthetic, just to create the desired image of ourselves in the heads of other people. Smoking cigarettes for example - when I was in high school, I watched Peaky Blinders - because in postmodernity our egos form and break quickly, because we lack grand-narrative identities, and perhaps because

humans are highly emphatic creatures, it's not un-
common for us to integrate fictional characters'
personality into our own identity - and so I smoked
because it was cool. Someone's aesthetic can be
sad, or cringe, and so we consciously shape our
unconscious behaviour patterns to see the world
in certain ways and hence receive a certain kind of
response.

As I mentioned above, being cringe requires a lot
of courage - but what for, exactly? For attention,
for fun, out of boredom, as an artistic or political
statement?

In anarchist communities, black garments are a
popular (though obviously not universal) aesthetic
- one interpretation could be that they're mourning
for their souls lost to materialism and capitalism in
postmodernity - yet, to me, postmodernity is not
the funeral but the cradle of our souls - once we
are nothing, we can become anything. We so often
mistake our identity (ego) for the soul. So many
people feel the void and try to resist it, instead of
fully giving oneself to it.

It's important to note that we can't really be sure
that materialist capitalism is the only way societies
can handle postmodernity.

< | >

When I read "How to Win Friends and Influence People," the corporate Bible on how to model your behaviour in order to make others like you, help you, or generally develop positive feelings towards you, the first two weeks I was stunned. This book, along with many others (including, for example, Anton Szandor LaVey's "Satanic Bible"), provide insights on applied psychology. Being aware of which behaviours spark empathy in humans, we can manipulate them for our own benefit. The results were palpable, yet after some time I started questioning the morality of such approach: am I not tricking other people into liking me, have I not become a people-pleaser ready to do anything for the other person to get personal benefits, and am I being dishonest?

For some time after that, I was an avid opponent of such practices. Beware the zeal of the convert, so they say. I saw manipulation, especially such subliminal use of applied psychology - yet alongside mass-media propaganda and so on - as a menace to individual liberty. Though I accept psychological egoism (the theory that all human actions are motivated by self interest, e.g. when you help somebody you actually do it to make yourself feel better etc.),

I found the term largely misleading, as it confuses ego with the soul. To me, the soul encapsulates the entire narcissistic spectrum (selfish Narcissus on the one hand, selfless Echo on the other), and hence we humans are capable of any behaviour and it's up to us to decide which road we take.

The more I dug into morality and the nature of reality, the meta-ironic nature of all human actions and their purely subjective judgement, the question of whether applied psychology methods for one's own benefit are honest, instead of being part and parcel of my meditations, became just a tiny fragment of this philosophical notion - namely, is any social performance honest? There are many factors one might take into consideration, such as whether the audience believes the performance is genuine, whether the performer themselves believe in the honesty of their performance, to what extent the performer is aware of the theatrical aspect of their performance, and so on. The easy answer to this is: there is no easy answer. The more aware you become of all these nitty-grittty details of our social lives, the more you grasp how very little we actually know. Asking a question only stirs more questions to arise. Is everything we do *acting*? If no, how can we tell if a manipulatory behaviour is a conscious or unconscious one, or maybe a learned skill? If we're all but actors on the societal stage, playing by the rules no one has ever discussed, rules that developed through social construction, the development of history, and mass media, what is the point in living, and why should we even engage and spend our energy on these performances - here, the range of social performances encapsulates all areas of human life: from professional environments to the personal spaces of our family homes.

Having taken a large detour through the implications of social performance, let us once again get back to the art of cringe. The realisation that nothing we do is *genuine* may lead to depression, drowning one in nihilism. On the flipside of this card, i.e. anti-nihilism, this approach teaches us that, yes, nothing matters and it's all a game, so we might as well play with it. At some point you face the fact that you won't find the answers to your questions, that you won't find the truth - but does it really matter?

After a year of living off-the-grid, I decided to get back on social media and play around with people's minds. I no longer asked myself whether it's moral, or what the intent behind my actions is. I stopped caring *why* and focused on action just for the hell of it (of course, as I mentioned, *not caring* is also a form of response one wants to get from the others, but you get my point). Hence, my few-month intense adventure with cringe started. I played around with Instagram posts and memes, TikTok videos, and so on. In a form of digital divine mania, I led my social media accounts in a way that for most people and at the first glance would be identified as mental illness, substance abuse, or a simple idiocy. And I didn't have to wait long until I started getting feedback: "Is he alright? What's wrong with him? Isn't he taking too much of that LSD?"

How entertaining - and satisfying - it was to see an immediate response to my actions. Fundamentally, the paranoid question that pops up in people's heads is why would anyone risk their social stance, why embarrass oneself - purposefully or not. The answer is: because it's fun. Because faced with the futility of human existence and caught up in a strange conundrum between suicide and a love for life, some find that there's nothing left but try to enjoy the short time we've got on this planet.

I recorded myself doing a make-up tutorial using Nutella instead of cosmetics, pretending I'm throwing up, or taking a shit. I posted intentionally unattractive pictures of myself, or edited them to look ridiculous, and so on. They were all in contrast to e.g. stories from my absolutely normal everyday life, only adding to the confusion and mixing "reality" with fiction (is that his personal or artistic account?). I think that the best impression was on the people who weren't directly in touch with me, so they couldn't juxtapose the digital and physical realities and verify either one. (Surely, even when I did meet people in person I sometimes behaved in a sort of manic way, just to make them all the more confused.)

By now I'm done with that period in my life and I've deleted most of my cringeposts. It was fun. Did it teach me anything? Did it teach *anybody* anything? Maybe. It's not up to me to decide, or even know if my actions had any effect on others (like showing them the division between self and ego, showing them how distanced I am to my self-image, and so on). And frankly, I don't care.

<|>

Praising God - distancing from ego, submitting to the absurd, faith in/becoming the void; all-forgiving God - the capacity of the unconscious to break the chains of trauma, defy the labels of psychology, the omnipotent creative machine of the subconscious that has the power to forgive (acceptance), to make new, to experiment and break rules beyond the limited "perceivable" human reality

One can never be fully egoless (if through *ego* we understand an individual's presentation of self in social situations). As long as we interact with the physical world, regardless of our level of asceticism, we do so through a certain behaviour, gestures, expressions. We can see egolessness as the void, the nothingness with infinite potential, and in this sense it exists only in the metaphysical realm, beyond this palpable world, as the sublime object of identity. Even a Buddha or (a) Christ represent(ed) their selves through a certain ego (a finite production of the infinite unconscious).

Astrology is a science - hence a framework - like any other. Though it successfully ties esoterism with hard-data research in some spheres, it still can give one only a limited view of reality. But, knowing how ideologies function, astrology does create the illusion of being *woke* and *aware*, leaving those into spirituality trapped only in a different kind of illusion. Here, astrology's sin is similar to that of modern psychology - in its attempt to understand, it only pigeonholes and puts labels on people, rather than embracing their potential for change. And surely, language is yet again at the bottom of the dispute (for what does it mean to be *hard-working*, who decides what *good-hearted* people do, and so on), distorting the image alongside our limited human perception, social constructs.

After ego death, one's life becomes art - since it's a simulation, we can mould it to convey a certain message, and that's how a human can be a piece of art.

III

THE INTERNET

cum isn't funny anymore

THE INTERNET

Why do rockstars grab girls' and boys' asses, spit on the ground and fart, burp, or dress edgy - because they can, because that's what people would like to do in public so much but don't/think they can't (is it desired just because it's prohibited - not really, but might be) (not everybody would like to but everyone technically can but doesn't - if it was free to do it, some people would do it, and some don't - just like you're free to eat ice cream for breakfast) because they're slaves (subjects) to societal implications of what's *decent* or *acceptable* - other reasons: just to break the rules and norms, raising controversy (to touch upon a social issue, gain publicity, and so on), creating a persona (in e.g. divine mania)

I love tricking people into thinking I'm a dumb piece of junkie shit for no reason!

After the Great War, art had no meaning. In late-capitalist postmodernity, nothing has any meaning.

Everything is a meta-ironic "being," whose existence's only property is "nothingness," "lack."

<|>

Let's say I make a meme about Millennials. So either
my intention is to mock Millennials, or I can mock
the fact that the memes about Millenials got popular
recently, or I may just notice the trend, or come up
with an original idea, but don't mean anything at
all. In the last case, it's a matter of something being
funny not because it conveys an underlying, comedic
message, but solely because it exists.

The way that groups form on the internet is somehow
revealing to me. If you look at the fanbases or interest
groups - usually on various social media platforms
- they rise and fall, their core is fluid, their activity
often based on voluntary input of a group's members,
their only given is that they're ever-changing. The
obvious drawback is that one tends to surround
oneself with people of similar opinions and hence
end up in a confirmation bubble whence our views
are rarely challenged - but does it have to be the
case? Yes, this disadvantage has been mentioned
time and time again, but is its scope really so vast?
In 2016, we've seen how social media platforms
and profiling users can be a tool of manipulation

(Cambridge Analytica scandal (just google it if you don't know)), yet it was by no means a grassroots undertaking; on the contrary, it was an external act of a sophisticated ad campaign. Cambridge Analytica has so far taken plenty of damage from whistleblowers online and its reputation undeniably diminished, but what about all those other gurus who want to monopolise the internet and seize control of the way we use it - Facebook and the rest of Silicon Valley? It's nothing new to say that Big Data is all into censorship of content they find 'inappropriate' according to their 'community guidelines'. Which one of us holds the right place to deem something offensive? Perhaps the creators of those social media platforms themselves... What can we do with it? Maybe we don't have to do anything. Social media platforms, they rise and fall, like everything these days. Despite all of the chaos around and inside it, we don't really need bureaucracy to wrap our heads around the internet. Among my generation, who are now entering adulthood, we can smell a soft scam from the way an email is written, we can navigate through technology instinctively, and we feel very comfortable in this digital mess.

In new grassroots organisations, such as Fridays for Future, the idea of a structure-less form of organisation is holding a key role. With the exclusion of

Greta Thunberg, who was (to some, still is) more of an inspiring symbol than a leader (for she hasn't particularly *directed* any decisions of the organisation, nor has she pushed for a unified agenda across local branches), the movement has achieved its egalitarian goals quite well. A leader-less group is not by definition chaotic; it's democratic, with *all* of the people involved, instead of a chosen few. FFF operates on direct democracy, with local, federation-like groups, which then have their (for the lack of a better word) representatives on national and international levels. Surely, some hierarchies form - and as some lobster fanatics remind us time and time again - they are natural in the animal kingdom. But how can we not see something sophisticatedly wicked in our current, representative "democracy?" Both the internet and FFF (both of which are inter-twined) show us that hierarchies form naturally in a fluid manner. Just like the mythical, Millenial alpha male has been debunked (and was meta-mocked for quite a long period of time, relatively to the longevity of memes) as another narrow-minded framework of looking at people, so is Generation Z (along with other generations of course, yet not in such a widespread way) gradually deconstructing all past forms of authority, rejecting traditional systems of dependencies, and embracing the postmodern chaos. So, in FFF, hierarchies are flexible, somewhat

44

artificial, and temporary - those holding a "high" status, e.g. attend international activist meetups, can be thrown down from the pinnacle at an instant, if only the rest of the group decides that it's in the organisation's best interest - and furthermore, the one who has committed a flaw is rarely stigmatised (I've never came across any such situation (which I know is not the best validation of opinion, but who cares, it's my goddamn book)) but only "degraded" (which, again, is not something particularly downplaying).

The internet, to me, is a profound expression of our human nature - without borders, beyond structure, pure chaos. I imagine society after the fall of capitalism as following very similar rules: no rules.

Some will call the vision Utopian. Since when are we calling democracy - *real*, direct democracy - a Utopia? Aren't these the very values already at the heart of the Western society (I use 'Western' as a simplification, as there is no distinctive 'Western society' today) but, instead of being raped by politicians and abused by corporations, actually implemented? And to you non-believers, you right-wing skeptics, you neo-liberal censors: look around! We already are chaos. And this chaos is like nothing humanity's ever seen. It will proceed regardless how much you pray to your weak, silver-haired God. It will smash borders no matter which flag you wipe your ass with. It will say anything it wants to say and it won't be cancelled. It will break everything down and push us to a breakthrough, and it's already happening. The process is only accelerating. See you in a new world, soon.

<|>

Neo-liberals are all for taxing the rich to combat economic inequality and fight climate change, which perhaps would work in a perfect capitalist world without corruption and manipulation. For where would the money go? Would it not go back to the hands of the same rich people? Back to the corporations, who hide their ruthless profit-oriented exploiting strategies behind slogans like "creating jobs" and "strengthening the [name of a nation] economy." Make America great again, huh? Who is America in this virtue-signalling vicious cycle, where nothing is true and the fight for basic human rights seems doomed for failure?

<|>

The internet's played a huge role in - basically - fucking up everything we knew about culture, society, maybe humanity itself. I like to go on with this analysis by taking a look at generations. So, in the pre-Boomer era, civilisation-wide (interpret *civilisation-wide* according to your preferences, I don't care really) we had a strong sense of what is *true*, what's *right* or *appropriate*, and that's how boomers still see the world. Then, with Gen X came punk rock as a continuation of the hippie's countercultural spirit, which ended more or less with the fall of Berlin Wall in 1989, soon before Millenials took over the mantle. They were the ones who grew up when the internet started to become more and more influential, those still looked down upon by the public as a niche medium for niche people to form niche groups. Additionally, those were also the times when the housing industry started to grow. Then came Gen Z, so the generation that's entering the job market right now. In comparison to the older generations, Gen Z uses the internet and technology intuitively. The tables have turned, and we no longer look up to older generations for guidance. The world is changing rapidly, and it's not controversial to observe just how often parents ask their kids how to use this or that device. The pace of change is so rapid that the council of the elderly no longer hold authority. The differences in mentality are stark and quite easy to see, and they are to change politics and society forever. While Millenials pushed for gay marriage and gay rights, Gen Z comes with (not so) brand-new ideas about gender and identity altogether. As concerns housing, while Millenials would get depressed about how difficult it is to get a real estate of one's own, Gen Z don't even think about this.

<| >

Social media algorithms and the development of technology, especially artificial intelligence, have developed exponentially at a rate never before seen in human history. Our phones are tracking devices, and our behaviour online is a way for advertisers to categorise us and deliver us just the right content, pre-tailored to our "needs" and interests, creating a reality bubble that traps us in communities aimed at instilling us in our beliefs intead of challenging them.

The algorithms know your tastes, and the entertainment tools - face filters etc. - are nothing but an open source research base for AI case studies, eg. for facial recognition. Every time you consume mass media, you're teaching artificial intelligence - which in itself is harmless, but in the hands of the powerful people it is likely to become a tool for mass terror, in a technocratic world of surveillance, whence we're sold the lie of individual freedom. Yes, we are free to choose, but are we free to choose the choice?

Today's mass media is a simulated reality. The postmodern condition is only accelerating with the internet, and as our social media accounts are digital simulations of us humans, our human lives then become simulations of that simulated reality. Just like one of the French postmodern thinkers said, sex doesn't exist. When people have sex today, what they do is simulate the behaviours they've seen so many times in pornography, which in itself is a simulation of the sexual intercourse. Hence, sex is a simulation of a simulation, while *the real thing* is a long-forgotten daydream. Apply this theory to other areas of daily living - eating out, partying, dating - and you quickly notice how what we do in "the real world" is a copy of the imagery we've been spoon-fed by mass media over decades. Our families are simulations of sitcoms, the way you walk is a mimicry of your favorite television show's main character, the commodities you chase; the things you think you want, are just examples of what you've been told you need. Each industry, each company has to create a demand for their product - this simple marketing rule taught in university classrooms is taken as a given, to the extent that we no longer see the wickedness of the capitalist machine.

The French thinker Deleuze in the 1970s developed a theory that we are entering, what he called, a society of control. Whether it's "good" or "bad" depends on how we look at it - control grants people security and security is the fundamental value for a society as big as ours to thrive, *or* for humanity to blossom, individual and/or collective liberty should be the paramount value... This I leave for you to decide. Yet, what I can do is provide you with a few insights and observations of how this process of permeating and ubiquitous control has become so common that we no longer perceive it as control. Our phones are a versatile example, as these devices has taken over a large part of our daily lives in just a few decades. Sure, you don't *have to* have a phone, but you do. Technology is present in every sphere of our lives: at work, at home, used for communication or entertainment, storing massive amounts of data on our preferences, geo-location history, and so on - but we all know that, don't we? Just pointing it out seems like a cliche: it's common knowledge that Big Data breaches our privacy and that supervision is getting tougher, but all we do is shrug our shoulders. Why? Well, it's easier, and we're quick to voluntarily give away our liberty and/or privacy in the name of comfort.

What to do then? Go off the grid and stop using

technology? We are technically free to choose that, but the price is sacrificing our social relations (in today's standards), so that's not really much of a choice - maybe for a few individuals, with no impact on the massive scale.

This is an illusion of free choice - imagine you have a choice between answers a) and b). Yes, you're free to choose between a) and b), but you're not free to choose the question, you're not free to choose the answers (there might be more possible ways to answer a question than just a) and b)), and what is more, maybe you don't even want to answer this questions at all?

Another example that Noam Chomsky used in an interview:

Interviewer: "You don't have to go to work. You're free to choose."

Chomsky: "Yes, you're free to starve."

Sure I am a bit skeptical of those intellectuals and theorists who spend most of their lives at universities and don't have too much in common with the working class, with their sweaty foreheads and sore feet, but anyway-

So going off the grid is the best counter-cultural

thing you can do: do not participate. But here, nota bene, it's not a problem of technology in itself. It's a matter of priorities. After Nietzsche heralded the death of God, it took a whole century of people trying to replace their divine figure: with political figures, extremely exclusive and prejudiced ideologies, and - in the end - with money and technology. I don't imagine a post-revolution society as a milk-and-honey utopia - we're still people, after all - but one that celebrates humanity atop of all, for whom technology and money are tools to serve and help us (each other), not the other way round. Going back to nature doesn't mean giving up on technology altogether, but rather using it in a more humane way. In a more human way.

Fuck me, I say, fuck me sevenfold. Again: a matter of priorities. We've got all the science and resources to provide all humans with shelter and sustenance. I am currently in a position where I experience the power imbalance first hand: the wealthy class discussing business innovations no one cares about or needs over a glass of champagne on the one hand, and filthy, rodent-plagued streets with homeless people begging and defecating on the pavement on the other. Seeing the amount of food and generally resources wasted every day is heartbreaking. We must question the status quo and the general ideology of personal gain, come to understand that our individual powers are indeed social powers, and nip the separation between the individual and society in the bud to take the necessary steps to construct an emancipatory society that cherishes freedom and humanity. Progress is a socially determined process that should benefit humanity as a collective, united body, rather than the rat race for capital. Justice, equity, and basic living conditions for the inhabitants of our planet - those values define liberalism in theory, yet in late-capitalism they're just ideas whose illusion is to be upheld over actually executing them.

Though William S. Burroughs' "Naked Lunch" holds no literary value, it was a crucial against censorship. It talked about gay sex and heroin, topics thought of as taboo in the 1950s. It's impact was substantial - decades later, social issues are discussed more freely. Also, writing something like "Naked Lunch" - a piece without structure, defying codes of what a book should be - shows that something like this *can* exist. A friend of mine once said, "If you ever write something like Naked Lunch, you should be ashamed of yourself." It seems to me that memes hold a similar role. In their simplicity, they push the boundaries of taboo (cum, racism, sex, disgust, etc.)

and prove that anything *can* exist.

That, to me, is the ultimate meta-ironic value of internet art.

Afterword

This little book is my last attempt at philosophy and non-fiction writing... for now. Lately, it's been more and more difficult to gather my thoughts into any comprehensive narrative, hence the style of my chapbooks (i.e. You Only Die Twice, troit errs, and CUNT*) is rather loose and/or changeable. Writing these pages was more about getting my thoughts out of my head rather than trying to explain anything to anyone.

My idea behind the chapbooks was influenced by a collection of diary thoughts by Andy Warhol published by Penguin. I thought it was a good format, and so I did it, without thinking too much. It might be true that those cheap chapbooks sold only because they had Warhol's name on the cover. But like I said, I wrote it for myself rather than for anybody else. Sure, people don't give a shit about philosophy, especially in such a free-form packaging.

To me, however, writing is therapy - a way of releasing my suppressed thoughts and emotions. And that's a good enough reason to start typing.

ilysm,

<|>

About the Author

after a failed suicide attempt, dada purged his old life and devoted himself to interdisciplinary art. his literary work includes fiction, poetry, and philosophy, alongside music and film productions. both an observer and an active part of the youth culture, dada's projects cover social issues closest to his own experiences, such as the bad mental health epidemic and substance abuse. born in east-central europe, after a year of hitchhiking, writing, and meditation, dada now lives in berlin and works on new projects.

instagram: @ickbindada

Also by dada

ilysm
When you stand on the final frontier of teenage angst and no road seems to be just right, trying to follow your own way may eventually put you face to face with the void. Fill it with an impossible love fantasy, a transcendental passion for music, or escapist drugs and alcohol? In this ignorant universe, on this hopeless planet, and in this filthy city, everything you see burns in front of your eyes, everything you smell reeks of misery, and nothing you hear makes any sense. Trauma pins you down to the ground, staining your leather jacket, and doubt tears your little rebel heart out up from your ribcage. Self-sabotage, therapy, suicide... Freedom?

DON'T BOTHER WITH ME
a collection written at the turn of 2021, it will take you on a journey through Europe, a journey through the soul, a journey through the fluctuations of both the inner and outer lives

Early Short Stories 2018-2020
tales of psychomachia, mourning, & filth written by dada in the pre-debut era.

You Only Die Twice

"You Only Die Twice" is a chapbook containing scraps of essays, bits of thoughts, and remnants of meditations on the meaning of one's identity, spirituality and God, and what it means to be free. Going through the pages like walking through the twisted corridors of dada's mind, the book covers an analysis of Gen Z's digital world, the subconscious power of dream manifestation, and reality construction.

troit errs

A collection of loosely-interwoven thoughts and reflections on the impact of money on our consumerist, late-capitalist society, the twisted and uncharted nature of love, and the perversive ways we seek control. Transcending the boundaries between fact and fiction, *troit errs* is a philosophical piece of art. Digging deep or staying into the surface, this book is a journey through the analyses of the human condition in a world of technology, surveillance, and a spiritual revolution.

its just a life
dada's second collection of poetry, to be published soon

Printed in Great Britain
by Amazon

80486938R00037